Grizzly
Bears

Other titles in the Returning Wildlife series include:

Returning Wildlife

Grizzly Bears

John E. Becker

KIDHAVEN
PRESS™

THOMSON

GALE™

San Diego • Detroit • New York • San Francisco • Cleveland
New Haven, Conn. • Waterville, Maine • London • Munich

THOMSON

———— ✦ ————™

GALE

To the memory of my dad, the "Bear."

© 2003 by KidHaven Press. KidHaven Press is an imprint of The Gale Group, Inc., a division of Thomson Learning, Inc.

KidHaven™ and Thomson Learning™ are trademarks used herein under license.

For more information, contact
KidHaven Press
27500 Drake Rd.
Farmington Hills, MI 48331-3535
Or you can visit our Internet site at http://www.gale.com

LIBRARY OF CONGRESS CATALOGING-IN-PUBLICATION DATA

Becker, John E., 1942–
  Grizzly bears / by John E. Becker.
    v. cm. — (Returning wildlife)
Summary: Discusses the history, characteristics, behavior, and habitat of the grizzly bear including population decline and recovery and conservation efforts.
Includes bibliographical references (p.   ).
  ISBN 0-7377-1534-0 (hardback : alk. paper)
1. Grizzly bear—Juvenile literature. [1. Grizzly bear. 2. Bears 3. Endangered species.]
I. Title. II. Series.
  QL737.C27 B434 2003
  599.784—dc21

                                                            2002154006

Printed in the United States of America

Contents

chapter 1

Gigantic Bear

As many as one hundred thousand grizzly bears may have been living in the western United States when white settlers arrived in the mid-1800s. The Native Americans who lived in grizzly country were fearful of the enormous bears but also believed they were related to people. Some tribes even referred to bears as great grandfather or uncle. Whites, however, only saw grizzlies as a menace that needed to be destroyed.

For more than one hundred years Americans shot, trapped, and poisoned grizzly bears until fewer than one thousand survived in the lower forty-eight states. After they were given protection by the Endangered Species Act in the 1970s grizzly bears began to recover. The recovery process has been slow, however, and grizzly bears are still a **threatened species**.

Bears Throughout History

Bears living in the world today all came from a common ancestor that first appeared more than 20 million years ago. Eight species of bears survive today: the sun bear of Asia, the giant panda of China, the spectacled bear of South America, the sloth bear of Asia, the Asiatic black bear, the American black bear, the polar bear, and the brown bear of Europe, Asia, and North America.

About 3.5 million years ago the ancestors of today's black bears came to North America. Brown bears, known in America as grizzly bears, first arrived here about fifty thousand years ago. Grizzlies once ranged from central

Mexico to the Arctic Ocean and from the Pacific Ocean to the Mississippi River. Today they live in scattered parts of the northwest United States, Canada, and Alaska.

Physical Characteristics

The name *grizzly* comes from the bear's distinctive silver-tipped fur. Grizzly bear fur is long and thick and varies from brown to black, gray, reddish brown, or blond.

Grizzlies are extremely large. Male grizzlies average 450 pounds, but a large male may stand eight feet tall (the height of an average ceiling) and weigh over 1,000 pounds (the same as five 200-pound men). Females weigh from 200 to 450 pounds.

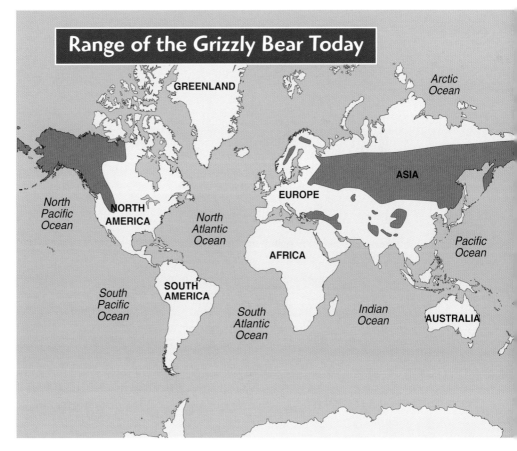

7

Standing on his hind legs, a male grizzly bear roars. Male grizzlies may stand as high as eight feet and weigh over one thousand pounds.

Grizzly bears are extremely fast for their size. A grizzly can easily outrun a person and is capable of keeping up with a horse for a short distance. It is estimated that grizzly bears can run faster than thirty-five miles per hour.

These bears are very powerful animals. A grizzly can kill a cow or bison with a single swipe of a mighty paw. Long, powerful claws prevent grizzlies from being good tree climbers, like black bears are. But grizzly claws are very effective for slashing prey and digging up burrowed animals and nutrient-rich plant stems.

The back teeth of a grizzly bear are good for grinding plants, and long **canine teeth** are effective at tearing flesh. Sharp teeth, combined with extremely powerful jaws, make grizzlies one of the most feared predators on Earth.

Grizzly bears use their long and powerful claws to slash prey and to dig.

A grizzly's sense of smell is stronger than a blood-hound's. Grizzlies can pick up the scent of rotting **carrion**—the remains of an animal that has died—two miles away. If a grizzly bear smells a human being it will usually avoid the person, which is why very few people are attacked by grizzly bears. The grizzly's sense of smell also helps it to identify other grizzly bears, especially during the breeding season.

Grizzlies see about as well as a person and hear slightly better than humans. They also hear high-pitched sounds that people cannot hear.

Grizzly bears make a variety of sounds to communicate with each other. They grunt, growl, and even make a loud roar. When two grizzly bears meet, the dominant bear will use body language and sounds to drive off the lesser bear. In that way painful, and possibly fatal, injuries are avoided.

Omnivores

Most of a grizzly bear's time is spent searching for food. A grizzly eats about thirty pounds of food per day. Grizzlies are **omnivores** but mainly eat plants such as grass, dandelions, clover, strawberries, roots, and seeds. They like honey and are not driven away from a beehive by stinging bees.

Meat—including large mammals such as bison, elk, and deer—also appeals to grizzly bears. If large game is not available grizzlies will settle for smaller animals such as ground squirrels and marmots. Grizzly bears will occasionally kill domestic livestock such as cows and sheep. Grizzlies are excellent swimmers and enjoy eating fish. They will sometimes fill up on ants, grubs, and moths. In addition, grizzly bears will eat carrion. Rotting animal carcasses appear to be a treat for the not-so-picky grizzlies. Human garbage is also a favorite source of food. Unfortunately, eating garbage has led to many human–grizzly

A grizzly bear catches a fawn. Grizzlies spend most of their time looking for food.

encounters in which people have been hurt, or killed, and grizzlies shot.

Grizzly Behaviors

Home ranges for grizzly bears can be quite large. In Yellowstone National Park individual male grizzly bears roam over an average of 750 square miles (male grizzlies range farther than females). One grizzly bear in Alaska traveled

11

over 2,200 square miles—more than the entire state of Delaware—in one summer. Both males and females allow other bears in the same territory.

In the fall grizzly bears go into a feeding frenzy to build up fat for their winter **hibernation**. A grizzly bear may put on one hundred pounds during that time. Shortly after the first snowfall in October or November, grizzly bears look for a den. They use either a cave or hollow tree or create a den by digging under the roots of a large tree. Inside they make a bed of grass, leaves, and tree branches and curl up for the winter. Grizzly bears may be in hibernation for ten weeks or up to seven months depending on the weather.

Mating and Reproduction

For most of its life a grizzly bear will live alone. But adult males and females find each other during the mating season in May or June. The couple will stay together for several days before once again going their separate ways. Occasionally males will fight over females, even to the death.

Female grizzly bears will give birth to one to four—usually two or three—cubs while in hibernation. The newborn cubs are born in January or February. They are born almost hairless, blind, and weighing only a pound. The helpless cubs nurse on their mother's milk. By spring, when the cubs leave the den with their mother, they weigh about six pounds. Cubs grow quickly, but only two out of three grizzly bear cubs survive to the age of two. Those that survive the first several months of life will grow quite large. By its first autumn a grizzly bear cub will weigh between sixty and one hundred pounds.

Cubs are playful and curious. They live with their mother for two or more years until she drives them away so she can breed again. Grizzly bears generally live from twenty to twenty-five years in the wild.

Mother grizzly bears are extremely protective of their cubs and are so aggressive that even adult male grizzly bears will usually be driven away from the cubs. Grizzly bears can be extremely dangerous. People who live or camp in grizzly bear country must be cautious not to surprise them and not to leave food or garbage in places that are accessible to the bears.

A mother grizzly stays close to her cub to offer protection. Grizzly cubs stay with their mother for about two years.

Habitat Loss

Grizzly bears have adapted to a wide variety of habitats. They can be found in mountains, forests, plains, **tundra**, and even dry semidesert areas. Grizzlies, like all animals, require habitat that includes shelter, water, and food. For grizzly bears the primary requirement is food. Today grizzly bears are only found in a tiny portion of their former habitat in Idaho, Montana, Washington, and Wyoming. Loss of habitat has been a major factor in the decline of grizzly bear populations.

chapter 2

Disappearance

No animals prey on adult grizzly bears, but grizzlies may be killed by another grizzly or, occasionally by a bison or elk who fights back after being targeted for an attack. Adult grizzlies may also occasionally die of starvation, avalanches, or forest fires. Young grizzlies are at the greatest risk and are killed by adult male grizzly bears, mountain lions, and wolves. They also die from disease, accidents, and starvation. These natural causes have affected the numbers of grizzly bears. However, people are the main reason grizzly bears are so rare in America.

Grizzly Bears and People

When Meriwether Lewis and William Clark explored the Louisiana Territory from 1804 to 1806 they encountered many ferocious grizzly bears. They killed more than forty bears, sometimes barely escaping with their own lives. Their exploration opened the West to white settlement, and their descriptions of the fearsome bears caused the new settlers to regard grizzlies as enemies that should be destroyed. When naturalist George Ord read the accounts of Lewis and Clark he gave grizzlies the scientific name *Ursus horribilis* (now *Ursus arctos horribilis*), or "horrible bear."

White settlers encountered many grizzly bears and killed every one they saw. Shooting them was a dangerous task, however, because it often took more than one shot to kill a grizzly. When single shot, muzzle-loaded rifles were replaced in 1848 with newly developed rapid-fire guns, hunters immediately had a great advantage over the

A growling grizzly is a frightening sight. American settlers killed many grizzlies out of fear.

bears. The new rifles allowed hunters to shoot large numbers of the bears, and from that point forward grizzly bear populations declined steadily.

Settlers discovered that grizzly bears were attracted to carrion. By using dead animals laced with poison the settlers were able to kill even more grizzlies.

Grizzlies were also trapped using dead animals as bait. During the 1800s a wide variety of traps were developed including huge, steel-jawed types which proved effective in capturing grizzlies.

Shrinking Habitat

When the United States acquired California in 1848 after the Mexican War, approximately ten thousand grizzly bears lived in the California territory. With the discovery of gold, thousands of Americans moved to California in 1849 to seek their fortune. Many of these new Californians established farms and ranches; farmers and ranchers slaughtered grizzly bears relentlessly to protect their livestock. One colorful character of that period was John Capen "Grizzly" Adams. Adams killed many grizzlies but gained fame by training two young grizzly bears, which he sometimes walked on a chain down the streets of San Francisco. Because of Adams and other grizzly hunters, by the late 1800s only a few grizzly bears survived in the mountains of California.

Despite the widespread slaughter, grizzlies living on the Great Plains actually increased in number during the late 1800s. At that time hunters were slaughtering bison by the thousands. Rotting bison bodies littered the plains, and grizzly bears benefited by eating the remains. Once bison herds were wiped out, however, hunters turned their attention to the grizzlies. During the last years of the nineteenth century the hunting of grizzly bears as "big game" animals became a popular pastime.

Over time, as more farms and ranches were established, grizzly bear habitat decreased. Farmers plowed under the prairie grasses and other plants that grizzlies depended on for their survival. First the Great Plains, then the foothills of the Rocky Mountains, and then mountain

Grizzly cubs play in prairie grass. Settlers destroyed much of this grass when they planted crops.

By the end of the nineteenth century, the grizzly bear population began to decline as more people moved into their habitat.

valleys were populated by people. Destruction of habitat affected the grizzly population as the nineteenth century drew to a close.

Government-sponsored programs to eliminate grizzly bears began late in the nineteenth century. At that time laws were passed that provided **bounties** for killing grizzlies in many western states. Thereafter, grizzly bear populations declined even more rapidly, and grizzlies became rare in the states where they still survived. In 1890 the last grizzly bear was killed in Texas.

Grizzly Bear Populations Continue to Decline

The campaign to destroy grizzly bears continued into the twentieth century, and by 1904 the average payment for a grizzly bear pelt was seventy-five dollars. That then represented a month's wages, which made the reward for killing a grizzly quite attractive. Many bounty hunters gained fame as "grizzly killers." One of the most famous of those hunters, Ben Lilly, killed three of the last grizzly bears in New Mexico in 1911. Before he died in 1936, Lilly claimed to have killed more than four hundred grizzly bears.

In 1915 the U.S. government began the Animal Damage Control (ADC) program to eliminate several types of dangerous animals. Under ADC, hunters were hired by the government to kill grizzly bears, wolves, mountain lions, and coyotes. Both bounty hunters and animal control agents were paid to eliminate the targeted animals. Soon grizzly bears began to disappear in state after state.

In 1922 a rancher shot the last grizzly bear in California. Even though the state flag of California still features a grizzly bear, no grizzlies have lived in the state for eighty years. Oregon lost its last grizzly bear to a government trapper in 1931. Colorado's last grizzly bear was killed in 1979.

Even after laws were passed in the 1970s giving protection to grizzly bears in the United States, **poachers** continued to kill grizzlies. The exact number of grizzly bears killed by poachers during the twentieth century will never be known, but wildlife officials suspect that the number is quite high.

Today one of the last strongholds for grizzly bears in the United States is Yellowstone National Park. But the illegal introduction of lake trout into Yellowstone Lake may harm bears there, too. In 1994 thousands of lake trout were discovered in the lake. Lake trout swim near the bottom and are not easily caught by grizzly bears. The lake trout prey on cutthroat trout, which swim close to the surface. Because cutthroat trout are an important food source for grizzlies the loss of these fish could spell trouble for the grizzlies of Yellowstone. Over the past several years U.S. Park Service employees have killed large numbers of

lake trout in Yellowstone Lake in an effort to prevent the disappearance of the cutthroat trout.

Headed Toward Extinction?

By the middle of the twentieth century grizzly bears were reduced to living in a very small part of their former range. Their survival depended upon the actions of concerned people—and many individuals, private organizations, and government agencies responded to the challenge.

chapter 3

Grizzly Bear Recovery

The grizzly bear sniffed the air and caught the scent of honey and bacon. The bear followed the scent to a strange-looking metal cylinder mounted on wheels. As the grizzly climbed in to reach the food a gate slammed shut, trapping him inside.

The next morning two scientists arrived in a pickup truck. They cautiously approached the cylinder and peered inside. The angry bear lashed out at them with its long claws.

The two men retreated for a moment but soon were busy at work. First, they weighed the trailer and the bear. When they subtracted the weight of the trailer they knew that the grizzly bear they had captured weighed 570 pounds—a medium-sized, aggressive male.

The next step was to temporarily put the bear to sleep, so one of the scientists injected the bear with a **tranquilizer** using a pole.

Within a few minutes the bear was quiet. The scientists carefully opened the gate and moved the grizzly onto the ground. Then they attached ear tags, took blood samples, and checked the bear's teeth to determine its age. Finally, they measured its paws and placed a radio collar around the bear's neck.

A few minutes later the bear began to stir. The scientists quickly packed up their gear and climbed back into their truck.

From a safe distance the men watched the bear stagger to its feet and wander off. As the bear disappeared into

Studying grizzly bears enables scientists to better understand how to help the population recover in the wild.

the woods the scientists listened to the signal from its col-lar—*beep, beep, beep.*

This bear is now part of an important study of the remaining grizzly bears in the United States.

Learning About Grizzlies

Throughout the early part of the twentieth century sci-entists knew very little about grizzlies. It was not until 1922 that in Mount McKinley National Park, Adolph Murie began the first scientific study of grizzly bears. At that time the study of grizzly bears was difficult and danger-ous. Later, in the late 1950s, the introduction of tranquil-izer drugs made the study of these bears much easier and safer. At first the drugs were given to the bears with nee-dles on the ends of sticks; tranquilizer darts were devel-oped later. Thereafter a captured grizzly bear could be given ear tags, which allowed scientists to easily identify the bear after it was released. The bear could also be given a medical examination.

In 1959 two brothers, Frank and John Craighead, began a long-term study of the grizzly bears in Yellow-stone National Park. The Craigheads took measurements to determine the height, weight, and age of the bears. They also took blood samples to determine the health of the bears.

Another important development gave the Craigheads the ability to learn where grizzlies traveled and the types of food they preferred. In 1961 scientists at the Philco Corpo-ration, working with the Craigheads, developed the first suc-cessful long-range radio collar for large mammals (radio collars had been used earlier on small mammals in Min-nesota). The sturdy collar consisted of a tiny radio transmit-ter that sent signals that could be picked up by a radio receiver several miles away. When a female bear was fitted with one of the collars and released, she became the world's first "radio bear." Using radio collars the Craigheads were able to learn about the behaviors of grizzly bears. Their work, and that of other scientists, convinced the federal government that urgent conservation measures needed to be taken to help the grizzly bear population recover.

Researchers examine a tranquilized bear and prepare to fit it with a radio collar. Long-range radio collars allow scientists to monitor grizzly bear behavior.

The Endangered Species Act protects grizzly bears. Killing a grizzly can lead to a fine or prison.

Grizzly Bear Conservation

Grizzly bears were given federal protection under the Endangered Species Act (ESA) in 1975, when they were listed as threatened in America's lower forty-eight states. The U.S. Fish & Wildlife Service (FWS) was the federal agency given responsibility for improvement under ESA. FWS has played a major role in protecting grizzly bears and their habitat: Anyone killing a grizzly bear may face a fine of twenty thousand dollars and a prison term of up to five years.

27

Glacier National Park in Montana is one of several Grizzly Bear Recovery Zones. The park can support a healthy population of grizzly bears.

In 1982 grizzly bear experts developed a recovery plan for the bears. Its goal was to reintroduce or maintain grizzlies in all states that could support a population of bears. The plan identified six ecosystems in the western United States as Grizzly Bear Recovery Zones:

- Yellowstone National Park and surrounding areas in Wyoming, Idaho, and Montana;
- Northern Continental Divide centered on Glacier National Park in Montana;
- Cabinet/Yaak Mountains in Montana and Idaho;

- Selkirk Mountains in Idaho and Washington;
- Northern Cascade Mountains in Washington;
- Bitterroot Wilderness and surrounding areas in Idaho and Montana.

Several federal agencies joined together to form the Interagency Grizzly Bear Committee (IGBC) in 1983. The following year the states of Wyoming, Idaho, Montana, and Washington were added to the committee. The goal of IGBC is to coordinate research and develop ways to help the grizzly bear. IGBC has been working on the recovery of Yellowstone grizzlies. As a result, those grizzlies have been surviving longer.

Reintroduction

The Bitterroot ecosystem has been suggested by IGBC as a possible area where grizzly bears could be **reintroduced**. Though grizzlies have not lived in this fifty-seven-hundred-square-mile wilderness area for sixty years, scientific studies indicate that the Bitterroot region would make good grizzly bear habitat. Because of its location in central Idaho, the Bitterroot area could also be part of an important link for grizzly bears living in Yellowstone to grizzlies living in other areas.

FWS, in 2000, accepted a plan to reintroduce grizzly bears. Known as the Citizen Management Plan, this program allows the citizens of Idaho and Montana to actively participate in the reintroduction of the grizzly bears, while allowing people living in the Bitterroot area to comment on the effect of grizzlies on their land.

One of the conservation organizations that played a major role in the development of the Citizen Management Plan was the National Wildlife Federation (NWF). NWF has been involved in conservation activities for grizzly

A Montana grizzly bear specialist lifts a grizzly cub out of a carrier. Someday, the cub will be released into a Grizzly Bear Recovery Zone.

bears for many years. It has helped focus attention on grizzly bears through public education. NWF has also taken legal action to ensure that grizzly bears are restored to healthy population levels.

Another conservation organization that helped to develop the Citizen Management Plan was Defenders of Wildlife. Defenders has also educated the public about the plight of grizzlies and administers the Bailey Wildlife Foundation Grizzly Compensation Trust. Many farmers and ranchers oppose grizzly bear recovery because these animals kill their livestock. Through the Bailey trust fund farmers and ranchers receive a fair price for any animals that are killed by grizzly bears. The compensation program has, therefore, helped to make livestock owners more accepting of the bears.

Slow Progress

While much progress has been made in grizzly bear recovery, the future of the species remains in doubt. The Bitterroot Recovery Zone, for example, has yet to be approved for grizzly bear reintroductions. And with the total number of grizzly bears in the lower forty-eight states hovering around one thousand, scientists caution that the next several years will be important to grizzly bear survival.

chapter 4

Unclear Future for Grizzlies

The huge grizzly bear waded into the rushing waters of the stream. The stream seemed to be filled with Yellowstone cutthroat trout.

The bear watched intently for a few moments until a large trout came too close. Instantly, the bear snapped up the trout in its powerful jaws.

A short distance away another grizzly bear appeared out of the woods and splashed into the stream.

The first bear paid the intruder little attention as it focused on the trout it was eating.

The two bears continued to ignore each other as they concentrated on taking advantage of the feast that nature had provided.

Grizzly bears flourish whenever they live in protected habitat and have an abundance of food. Unfortunately, grizzly bear habitat is disappearing and that continues to be the greatest long-term threat to the survival of grizzlies.

Obstacles to Overcome

The remote mountain wilderness areas of Wyoming, Montana, Idaho, and Washington are the only areas in which grizzly bears survive in the lower forty-eight states. Unfortunately, those same areas are now considered attractive places for people to build homes. Where homes are built, towns, shopping centers, and golf courses soon follow. Land developers also see grizzly bear habitat as the ideal setting for ski resorts. With each new development grizzly bears have less and less territory over which to roam.

As human populations increase in grizzly bear country, there are also more conflicts between people and grizzlies. Grizzly bears know that where they find people, they will usually find food. Despite the increased use of "bear-proof" containers, some bears continue to raid garbage cans, break into campers' tents, and, occasionally,

A group of grizzlies fish for trout in an Alaskan river. Grizzly bears thrive wherever there is an abundance of food.

attack people. These problem bears are captured and relocated to other areas. In many cases, however, even when these animals have been relocated hundreds of miles away, they somehow manage to find their way back. Bears that continue to be a problem are killed.

Encounters between bears and people are common in grizzly bear country. Here, a grizzly watches a human with curiosity.

Some people kill grizzly bears even when they are not causing a problem; poaching continues to be a serious problem for these bears. In most instances grizzlies are poached when a hunter happens upon one while hunting some other animal. Most hunters will pass the opportunity by, but some are unable to resist the temptation to kill the bear.

Poachers are not the only people keeping grizzly bears from increasing in number, however. Mining operators, timber companies, and real estate developers have all opposed grizzly bear recovery plans at one time or another. Some private citizens, fearful of grizzly bears, have also opposed having grizzly bears live in their areas. Since 1900 twenty-one people have been killed, and many others injured, by grizzly bears. Nevertheless, not every program for grizzlies has been opposed.

Restoration Projects

Scientists believe that there is an urgent need to establish **wildlife linkage zones** between the areas where grizzly bears live. The bears living in Yellowstone National Park, for example, are currently isolated and unable to breed with grizzlies in other protected areas. If that situation continues, **inbreeding** may become a serious threat. The Yellowstone to Yukon Conservation Initiative (Y2Y) is an innovative plan to link wildlife habitat in the Rocky Mountains from Yellowstone National Park to Yukon Territory in Canada. Over 270 agencies and organizations are working together to protect this unique environment for grizzlies and other wildlife through Y2Y.

Grizzly bears need large areas to roam through—without roads. Closing roads that crisscross grizzly bear habitat, therefore, is another high priority for wildlife managers. Many forest roads have already been closed in parts

Wildlife managers are closing roads in grizzly habitats to protect bears, such as this female grizzly and her cub, from traffic.

of grizzly bear country, and more are scheduled to be closed in the future. Where major highways cut through grizzly territory **wildlife crossings** have been built under the highway. These crossings allow wildlife to go from one side of the highway to the other without being hit by cars or trucks.

People are also finding ways to help grizzly bears by using other innovative strategies.

A Helping Hand for Grizzly Bears

A growing problem for grizzly bears is the decline of whitebark pine trees. The seeds found in the cones of these trees are an important food for grizzly bears. The seeds provide a valuable source of fat that the bears depend on during their winter hibernation. Grizzlies, therefore, feed on the seeds from mid-August to late fall and again in the spring when they emerge from hibernation. Unfortunately, a disease called white-pine blister rust, the mountain pine beetle, and a lack of forest fires have combined to cause a serious decline in whitebark pine

The National Wildlife Federation and Northwest Connections are two of the conservation organizations working hard to help the grizzly bear population recover.

Although the future of grizzly bears is uncertain, many plans are in place to ensure that conservation efforts continue.

trees across grizzly bear territory in America's lower forty-eight states. When grizzlies cannot find whitebark pine seeds to eat in higher elevations they come down nearer to where people live to search for food. Consequently, there are more conflicts between grizzlies and people.

One conservation organization, Northwest Connections (NwC) in Montana, is playing an important role in restoring whitebark pine trees. NwC, through its Wildlands Volunteer Corps, involves high school students in mapping the remaining stands of whitebark pine trees. This project is also helping to identify rust-resistant trees from which seeds will be collected to produce healthy seedlings. These seedlings will grow to be part of a healthy new whitebark pine community.

An innovative way to help grizzly bears is the Partners in Life program developed by bear biologist Carrie Hunt at the Wind River Bear Institute in Utah. Karelian Bear Dogs, highly trained and fearless, help teach grizzly bears to keep their distance from people and their property. Karelian Bear Dogs, red pepper spray, and rubber bullets all warn bears to stay away and stay wild. This helps save the lives of bears.

School children are also helping grizzly bears to recover. Organizations such as Brown Bear Resources in Missoula, Montana, give students the opportunity to "Adopt A Grizzly." When a student or school class adopts a grizzly they receive educational information about the bear they have adopted as well as a newsletter that helps them to keep up with grizzly bear recovery programs. Money from the adoptions goes toward research projects leading to the return of grizzly bears.

An Uncertain Outlook

Many people have worked tirelessly to help grizzly bear populations recover. The increase in the Yellowstone grizzly population from approximately two hundred in 1975 to over six hundred today is an example of how successful some of these conservation efforts have been. The number of grizzly bears in other areas remains low, however, so there is still a great deal of work to be done.

bounty: A reward given for the killing of a harmful animal.

canine teeth: The four pointed teeth located on either side of the upper and lower jaw.

carrion: Flesh of a dead animal.

hibernation: A state in which bodily functions such as breathing and heart rate slow down in cold temperatures, leading to inactivity.

home range: The territory over which an animal repeatedly travels, searching for food.

inbreeding: Breeding with closely related family members.

omnivore: An animal that eats both meat and plants.

poacher: A person who takes game or endangered animals illegally.

reintroduced: To introduce again, as in returning animals to areas from which they disappeared.

threatened species: Animals not in immediate danger of extinction, but whose population levels merit protection.

tranquilizer: Drug that causes drowsiness and sleep.

tundra: The vast, treeless plains of the arctic regions.

wildlife crossings: Underpasses or overpasses that allow animals to pass safely from one side of a highway to the other.

wildlife linkage zone: An area of continuous habitat that allows animals to move from one area to another.

Books and Periodicals

Eleanor J. Hall, *Nature's Predators: Grizzly Bears*. San Diego: KidHaven Press, 2002. Presents the physical characteristics, behaviors, and relationship of grizzly bears with people.

Gail Jokerst, "Fingerprinting Griz," *Wild Outdoor World*, November/December 2000. Examines the project in Glacier National Park using genetic fingerprinting to identify and follow the movements of grizzly bears in the park.

Janice Parker, *The Untamed World: Grizzly Bears*. Austin, TX: Raintree Steck-Vaughn, 1997. Describes the world of the grizzly bear including their habitat needs, social structure, and feeding behaviors.

Elizabeth Schleichert, "Grrrr-izz," *Ranger Rick*, February 1999. Describes the hunting behaviors and basic physical characteristics of grizzlies.

Alvin Silverstein, Virginia Silverstein, and Laura Silverstein Nunn, *The Grizzly Bear*. Brookfield, CT: Millbrook Press, 1998. Discusses the survival challenges facing grizzly bears today and describes the basic characteristics and behaviors of this threatened species.

Lynn M. Stone, *Grizzlies*. Minneapolis: Carolrhoda Books, 1993. Explores the world of bears with an emphasis on brown bears, their physical characteristics, and behaviors.

Organizations to Contact

Defenders of Wildlife
National Headquarters
1101 14th St. NW, Rm. 1400
Washington, DC 20005

(202) 682-9400

www.defenders.org

An organization dedicated to conservation of all native wild animals and plants.

National Wildlife Federation

11100 Wildlife Center Dr.

Reston, VA 20190-5362

(703) 438-6000

www.nwf.org

This organization supports conservation activities for numerous endangered species around the world with educational information, legal action, and restoration activities.

Northwest Connections

PO Box 1309

Swan Valley, MT 59826

(406) 754-3185

www.northwestconnections.org

A conservation and education organization concerned with involving local people of the Swan Valley in Montana in preserving habitat linkages.

Wind River Bear Institute

PO Box 307

Heber City, UT 84032

(435) 654-6644

www.beardogs.org

An organization committed to reducing human/bear conflicts through aversive conditioning.

Website

Brown Bear Resources (www.brownbear.org). An organization focused on educational activities and restoration strategies for grizzly bears.

Video

The Great Bears of Alaska. The Discovery Video Library, 1992. Follows the life style, food preferences, and habitat usage of a grizzly bear family in the Alaskan wilderness.

Acknowledgments

Lance Craighead, Craighead Environmental
Research Institute
Carrie Hunt, Wind River Bear Institute
Sterling Miller, National Wildlife Federation
Lori Monska, Columbus Zoo and Aquarium
Tom Parker, Northwest Connections
Laird Robinson, Interagency Grizzly Bear Committee
Chuck Schwartz, U.S. Geological Survey
Chris Servheen, U.S. Fish and Wildlife Service
Alicia Shelly, Columbus Zoo and Aquarium
Andrea Stephens, Northwest Connections
Bob Summerfield, U.S. Forest Service
Trisha White, Defenders of Wildlife

John E. Becker writes books and magazine articles about nature and wild animals for children. He graduated from Ohio State University in the field of education. He has been an elementary school teacher, college professor, and zoo administrator and has worked in the field of wildlife conservation with the International Society for Endangered Cats. He currently lives in Delaware, Ohio, and teaches writing at the Thurber Writing Academy. He also enjoys visiting schools and sharing his love of writing with kids. In his spare time, Becker likes to read, hike in the woods, ice skate, and play tennis.